THE H

The Hunt of Her Life
SEQUEL

The journey moves forward with Samantha's grandnephew

By Joseph A. Reppucci

About the book

Acknowledgments: This book is dedicated to my dear friend, the late Rev. Bruce T. Robb, a former resident of Quincy, Massachusetts, who served as pastor of the Preston Hollow Baptist Church of Preston Hollow, New York. Rev. Robb's friendship and spiritual guidance played an important part in many people's lives, including my own. My appreciation goes to Matthew Spencer, a newspaper/magazine journalist and native of Lexington, Massachusetts, and Maryellen Dever of Hingham, Massachusetts, a free-lance journalist and writer, who volunteered their services to edit and proofread this book. Thanks also go to Mark Mahoney of Whitman, Massachusetts, a graphic designer who volunteered his services to design the book's cover.

About the author: Joseph A. Reppucci of Lexington, Massachusetts, has worked as a reporter and editor for more than three decades on major daily newspapers in the Greater Boston area, including The Patriot Ledger of Quincy, The Telegram & Gazette of Worcester and The Evening News of Salem. He holds a bachelor's degree in journalism from Suffolk University in Boston, where during his senior year he was the editor in chief of The Suffolk Journal, a student newspaper which won acclaim for its quality from the Columbia University Graduate School of Journalism. He is a graduate of Lexington High School.

About the front and back cover photos, the interior photos and the book's design: The cutout photo on front and photo on back are of Samantha, a key character in the book. Both pictures were taken by the book's author at Willards Woods in Lexington, Massachusetts. All interior photos and the design of the book's interior are also done by the author.

Copyright © 2015 by **Joseph A. Reppucci**

All rights reserved. No part of this book may be reproduced without written permission from the author, except by a reviewer who may quote brief passages in a review with appropriate credits. No part of this book may be reproduced, stored in a retrieval system or transmitted in any form or by any means – such as electronic, mechanical, photocopying, recording or other – without written permission from the author.

Contents

Introduction: A new life with dogs 4

Chapter 1: Un-Lady-like 7

Chapter 2: It's super mom! 17

Chapter 3: The great awakening 27

Chapter 4: The singleton puppy 37

Chapter 5: Oh boy! 43

Chapter 6: A haven for bird dogs 53

Chapter 7: One dog, two worlds 63

Chapter 8: Physical and mystical 71

Introduction

A new life with dogs

A new era in my life with dogs had dawned with the birth of Samantha's grandnephew, Sampson, on April 30, 2010. The birth, which occurred a little more than two years after my beloved rescue dog's death on April 7, 2008, had advanced Samantha's bloodline to a new generation. This unique English Setter bloodline, which was started and cultivated in the 1990s by Michael Ryba of Brookfield, Connecticut, and his hunting friends in western Connecticut, had been in danger of dying out.

> **This singleton puppy's birth was a time of joy, but it also was a time of great transition. I would be traveling down a trail I had never gone down before.**

Sampson's birth was more than just a jubilant event. It was mystical. This puppy's birth coincidentally occurred on what would have been the 83rd birthday of my deceased mother, the person who passed on to me her love for dogs and animals. And the event was even more improbable because Lady, Sampson's mother, defied overwhelming odds by giving birth to a single puppy rather than a litter. English Setters normally have six to eight puppies, and occasionally they bear even more.

A new trail

This singleton puppy's birth was a time of joy, but it also was a time of great transition. I would be traveling down a trail I had never gone down before. For the first time, I would have two English Setters living with me in my small suburban house in Lexington, Massachusetts. My previous English Setters – Dancer, my first, Samantha and then Lady – had each lived alone with me. I had become accustomed to living with only one dog.

Samantha's urn is displayed on a stand in the living room at our house. Each day, I gently kiss it the very same way that I would peck her on top of the head each night while she rested on her bed and as I did for the final time on April 7, 2008, when she was allowed to peacefully "go to sleep." I shall carry on this ritual until I get the chance to again directly kiss her head on the other side of the Rainbow Bridge.

I was looking forward to watching Lady and Sampson carry on many of the traditions that I had established with Samantha, especially the daily hikes to view wildlife in the beautiful wooded parks and conservation areas in my hometown. But I also was a little nervous, because the birth of this singleton puppy was the beginning of a new adventure that could have many potential obstacles.

In many ways, I was unprepared for the upcoming journey, especially since my house was ill-equipped to handle a vibrant mother bird dog and her bursting-with-energy puppy. I faced a slew of questions. Where would the whelping box be located? How do I set up a safe room to create the proper environment to raise a puppy? How would these energetic dogs get enough activity? How could their desire to hunt birds be satisfied? And what about the nuances of dealing with a singleton puppy? How do I make up for Sampson's lack of siblings that would normally be around to play with him, comfort him and emotionally support him?

I also had never before dealt with a puppy from birth. I had no idea what my role would be with a mother dog and her singleton puppy. And what about when the puppy got a little older? How would Lady and Sampson interact? Would they get along?

A divided world

Different worlds also awaited Sampson. He was a bird dog living in a family atmosphere, yet he had a long list of champions in his bloodline tracing back to Grouse Ridge Kennels of Oxford, New York. Those champions included Grouse Ridge Will, the 1971 bird dog national champion and a member of the Bird Dog Hall of Fame.

This dichotomy raised further questions. Could Sampson be happy and true to his innate bird dog instincts while living in a family hiking environment rather than a hunting kennel? Conversely, would he become overwhelmed by the tug of those instincts, making him unhappy, frustrated and unable to adapt to family life?

Another new wrinkle also had been added. I had a male dog in the house for the first time. And, oh boy, what an unexpected topsy-turvy difference from dealing with the females!

The questions about the potential challenges and obstacles were many while I prepared to traverse a new trail in life with Lady and Sampson. The Hunt of Her Life *Sequel*, which focuses on Sampson's puppy days, is a look back at the graceful – and sometimes not so graceful – ways I coped with those difficulties and hurdles during my journey into the unknown.

Chapter 1
Un-Lady-like

A pitter-patter emanates from behind the kitchen stove, a friendly whisper reverberates in the living room and a porch screen door slightly creaks when it slowly opens.

And each muscle of Lady's body quivers while she intensely listens from a new whelping box in the kitchen. She is trying to determine if these household sounds represent an impending threat to her newborn puppy, Sampson. Mother dogs are normally quite protective of their litters, but Lady is even more vigilant than usual regarding this puppy's well-being. For this proud mom, Sampson is a precious pup. He is an only child.

In an instant, a gentle, mild-mannered, 40-pound English Setter with no history of aggression is ready to turn into a ferocious beast whenever she senses any possible danger for Sampson. And from cautious Lady's perspective, everything – and everybody – is a potential threat to her puppy until proven otherwise.

> **Lady would rest next to Sampson in the whelping box with her eyes slightly open, keeping constant watch for potential threats.**

A protective mom

Liz Mahoney, our longtime pet-sitter who had forged a strong bond with Lady while helping with her care for nearly a year, including when she was pregnant with Sampson, learned this lesson the hard way. Liz, a resident of neighboring Arlington, Massachusetts, was anxious to visit the newborn puppy, especially since Sampson was Samantha's grandnephew. For several years, Liz had helped with Samantha's care and was heartbroken when my once-in-a-lifetime rescue bird dog succumbed to illness a couple of years earlier at age 11. When Lady,

Samantha's distant cousin, arrived, Liz was thrilled and resumed her role as our pet-sitter.

"Hi Joe, I'm here," Liz said with excitement while she stood outside on the side porch entryway that leads into the kitchen where Lady was nursing Sampson. The 4-day-old puppy had yet to develop the ability to see or hear, and he was totally dependent upon his mother.

"The door's unlocked, Liz. Come on in," I replied.

The entryway's screen door softly creaked when Liz slowly opened it. She had one foot inside when an angrily barking Lady charged out of her whelping box and blocked Liz in the doorway, preventing her from coming into the kitchen. The normally sweet-demeanored Lady was prepared to fight to protect her pup from everyone, even her beloved pet-sitter.

A terrified Liz, holding a bag with toys in her left hand that included a red-and-orange stuffed toy dog for Sampson, stood motionless in the entryway.

"Lady, stay," I shouted while scurrying across the kitchen to calm my normally friendly bird dog and lead her back to the whelping box.

With Lady now resting comfortably with Sampson, Liz was able to slip into the adjacent living room, about 10 feet away from the whelping box. From there, we peered into the kitchen to watch Lady nurse Sampson.

Sampson appeared to have everything a puppy could want while he slept with Lady wrapped around him. Yet the scene looked a little lonely while he rested in solitude without litter mates. A short time later, I took the stuffed toy dog and put it in the whelping box. Sampson was just under a pound at birth and about 5 inches long, the length of a chipmunk. He fit in my hand. Now, four days after birth, he already had grown to about 9 inches and his weight had almost doubled. The plump puppy overflowed from my hand. But the 7-inch-long stuffed toy dog was the perfect size for Sampson to use as a headrest. He snuggled against it, rubbing his head on it as if it were a brother or sister.

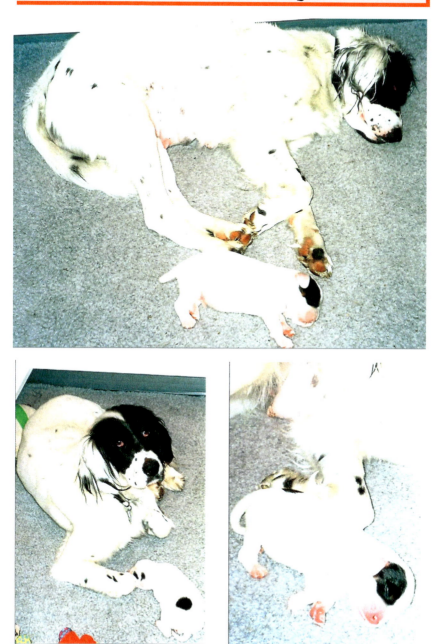

The ever-vigilant Lady keeps watch over Sampson. She uses her paw to stay in constant contact with her infant puppy.

With the help of our pet-sitter, the singleton puppy had found a "litter mate."

Not very neighborly

I realized that I should have been more careful when Liz arrived at the house, because a prelude to Lady's protective behavior had occurred a few days earlier. She had a hyper-vigilant reaction to a longtime neighbor's familiar, friendly voice. Jim Pates, the friend who witnessed Samantha's miraculous recovery from near death at Tufts University's Foster Hospital for Small Animals a little more than two years earlier, visited on the day that Sampson was born.

Lady had come to live with me in July 2009, and during the 10 months prior to Sampson's birth, she had spent many afternoons romping around Jim's backyard. We frequently would stop there to visit during our afternoon walks around our neighborhood.

Lady knew Jim well, but her mannerisms toward him during his visit to see the newborn puppy made it clear that she preferred he keep his distance. Jim quietly chatted with me in the doorway between the living room and kitchen, about 10 feet from the whelping box. As we watched, Lady kept her eyes fixed on Jim while she nursed Sampson.

"She's not going to let me get any closer," Jim said. "There's no way she's going to let anyone even think of harming that puppy."

But Jim was more than satisfied to observe the proud mother and her infant puppy from a short distance. "It's amazing how tiny he is," he said about Sampson. "I've never seen a newborn puppy, and I didn't realize they were this small."

To be precise, Sampson weighed 12.75 ounces at birth. And this singleton puppy would have an unlimited supply of nourishment available to him at all times since he had no siblings competing for his mother's milk. And he also had no brothers or sisters vying for Lady's attention. An unlimited supply of food, your mother's undivided attention and a warm whelping box seemed like utopia.

Sampson sleeps on a stuffed toy next to the white guardrail in his whelping box. Stuffed toys would become his "litter mates."

Yet without siblings for support, Sampson was emotionally alone with only a stuffed toy dog by his side.

Sleepless nights

Sampson may have had no siblings, but he did have a mother willing to unconditionally love him and protect him around the clock. Even at night, Lady would rest next to Sampson in the whelping box with her eyes slightly open, keeping constant watch for potential threats to her puppy. During the first few nights after Sampson's birth, she never seemed to be falling into a deep sleep, which concerned me. She had just gone through giving birth, and I was worried about her health.

On the fourth night after Sampson's birth, I started sitting in a chair near the whelping box until the wee hours of the morning to support Lady. The sense of security she felt with me nearby allowed her to finally fully close her eyes. On a couple of occasions, an exhausted Lady slept so deeply that she began to briefly snore. Sampson, still being an infant, had yet to develop a sense of hearing, so he was unaware of the snoring. But the throaty, snorting sound – which sometimes lasted in bursts of several seconds – sure kept me from napping in the nearby chair.

After a couple of weeks, Lady became more at ease at night. By this time, Sampson had developed the ability to hear and see. I no longer was needed in the nearby chair, and I returned to sleeping in my close-by bedroom.

For the next couple of weeks, Lady and I were able to squirrel away some badly needed sleep.

An uninvited guest

Sampson was slowly becoming a sentient puppy when he approached two weeks old. His newly opened eyes allowed him to observe his surroundings. He also was becoming responsive to the household sounds around him, including the soft classical music that had been playing in

Lady rests with her eyes slightly open to keep watch for potential threats to Sampson.

the background from the day he was born. He had no siblings, so I wanted to make sure the first sounds he heard around him were soothing.

The classical music also helped to comfort the ever-vigilant Lady, who was sleeping more at night but was still being extremely protective of her puppy. During the night, her collar tags often would jingle, an indication she was frequently lifting her head up while resting in the whelping box so she could look around the kitchen and living room.

On one particular night, the jingling became so persistent that I got out of bed and went to the kitchen to check on her and Sampson, who was now a bouncing 4-week-old puppy. Sampson was asleep and all seemed well, but Lady's eyes were fixated on the kitchen stove and her ears were raised. She appeared to be hearing some activity. I looked carefully around the stove, found nothing unusual and went back to bed.

On the following evening, I was standing barefooted by the stove – about 10 feet from the whelping box – preparing dinner when I momentarily heard a soft pitter-patter coming from next to it and felt something faintly brush against my foot. Suddenly, Lady came dashing from the whelping box and across the kitchen in pursuit of a small critter who scampered into the living room. The critter, which turned out to be a flying squirrel, was the reason why Lady had been closely watching the kitchen stove area during the previous night. It must have gotten into the house during the previous day by climbing down the living room chimney.

The commotion from Lady chasing the horrified squirrel around the furniture in the living room woke up Sampson. He became frightened by the noise and promptly began wailing for his mother, who was in full hunt mode. The scene would soon turn into pandemonium. The flying squirrel tried to find a safe haven by going up the stairway to the second floor with Lady hotly in pursuit. Lady appeared to have the squirrel cornered when it reached the top of the stairway and cowered next to the closed door. But the resourceful little guy climbed onto the banister and jumped into the living room below. Lady raced down the stairs to continue the pursuit. By now, a lamp had been toppled and an end table overturned. Oh, and of course, Sampson was in the whelping box still wailing – now even louder.

Lady snuggles with 6-week-old Sampson. She would continue being very protective of her puppy even when he got older.

I was unsure about what to do – other than panic – so I called the police for help, explaining my predicament to a mystified dispatcher. "I don't know if this is something we can help you with sir," he politely said while Sampson's cries had turned into shrieks in the background. "This isn't really a police matter."

"Please sir, I'm really in a bind here," I told the dispatcher while a second lamp and end table came crashing down in the living room.

Apparently, the combination of Sampson's persistent wails, the crashing lamp and my pleading voice convinced the extremely patient dispatcher that I truly was in a sorry state.

"I can't promise anything, but I'll call the patrol car," he said. "Sometimes, if it's a quiet night, an officer is willing to help out with these kinds of unusual situations."

A short time later, one of Lexington's finest, wearing huge mitts, arrived at my messy house. In addition to the overturned end tables and toppled lamps, the chair cushion, couch cushions and pillows were scattered across the floor. By now, Lady had chased the flying squirrel into the back bedroom, and I had shut the door.

The police officer – hearing Sampson's cries, observing the mess around the house and seeing the overwhelmed look on my face – tried to assure me that everything would be OK. "What a beautiful dog," he said while looking at Lady, whose eyes were fixated on the back bedroom door. "Wow, she's definitely going to make sure that squirrel doesn't get anywhere near her puppy. I think I'm going to have her help us out."

A plan of action

The officer then devised a plan to remove the flying squirrel from the house. He would chase the squirrel from the back bedroom. The squirrel would be forced to flee through a hallway that runs between the living room and kitchen, then into the kitchen and out the kitchen door. But we had to make a few preparations before implementing the plan. The kitchen door leading to the yard was opened, Sampson was put into a small kennel and placed in the living room, and Lady and I positioned ourselves in the living room doorway to discourage the squirrel from choosing that route instead of going through the kitchen.

A few moments later, the officer – wearing his large mitts – went into the bedroom, moved around some furniture and the nervous squirrel soon made a dash into the hallway. He initially tried to turn into the living room, but saw Lady, so he raced into the kitchen, where Lady promptly chased him out the open door and into the yard.

Lady's message was clear: Until Sampson could fend for himself, nobody – other than me – would be allowed to get near her precious pup. And that included a beloved pet-sitter, a longtime friendly neighbor and especially a pitter-pattering flying squirrel.

Chapter 2
It's super mom!

Lady let out an ear-piercing squeal while awkwardly sitting in the middle of the living room floor with her weight shifted onto her tail and her hind legs extended forward, outward and dangling. She looked like a person leaning back on a reclining chair with each leg draped over the arms of the chair.

"Easy girl," I said while rubbing her feet and ankles in an attempt to determine the source of her pain. Lady let out another yelp when my hand moved higher onto her right thigh toward her hip. Her right thigh muscle had gone into spasm from overuse and her hip showed signs of a strain.

> I had a premonition that something or somebody that I needed to see awaited me at Samantha's favorite stomping ground.

Lady's injury, which would heal after about 10 days of twice-a-day massage that would be followed with the application of soothing cold packs to reduce swelling, was quite predictable. This middle-aged bird dog had been following an intense daily activity routine for four months since Sampson's birth.

Double duty

Starting at 7 a.m. each day, 6-year-old Lady would spend nearly three hours in the backyard teaching her puppy about the art of pointing at birds and flushing them from the bushes. At midday, she insisted on going with me to the park, where we would spend an hour or two hiking. Then, in the afternoon, she would spend hours chasing, wrestling and playing with the bouncing boy.

Lady had morphed into a super mom. She wanted to spend every possible moment with Sampson. She had a special bond with this boy.

Work time!

Lady and Sampson sniff out birds and critters in our backyard. The proud mom would spend hours every morning teaching hunting techniques to her son. Sampson, who is 6 weeks old here, became an enthusiastic student who was eager to learn the finer points of being a bird dog.

Playtime!

Lady and Sampson enjoy playing and running in our backyard. After spending mornings teaching her son how to point at birds, this nonstop mother would use afternoons to make sure her puppy, who is 6 weeks old here, got plenty of exercise.

He was her only puppy. She enthusiastically filled the dual role as Sampson's motherly mentor and playful litter mate while continuing as my hiking partner. She had refused to slow down until a sore hip forced her to finally rest.

A mom to all critters

Lady's maternal instincts went well beyond her deep affection for Sampson. It would soon become evident that this proud mom possesses an affinity for all newborns, including the offspring of wildlife.

This was never more evident than on a springtime afternoon while Lady and I were walking through the Lexington Center area, where the wide sidewalks are lined with thick shrubbery that make an ideal hiding place for birds. Sometimes Lady could take up to an hour to walk just a few blocks. Her skillful, methodical way of constantly poking her head in and out of the shrubs to flush out the birds took patience. Lady would somehow find the hiding bird no matter how much time it took.

Lady, who has always been particularly fascinated with some azalea shrubs on the lawn between the town hall and police station, seemed especially focused on this spot during this walk. A dozen 5-foot high bushes form a 15-foot circle around a towering flag pole. Lady likes to squirm through a space between two of the bushes to gain access to an open area around the flag pole, where she can then poke her head into the backsides of all the bushes to flush out birds.

"There must be some kind of a bird's nest in there," said Lexington resident Dave Poynton, who spotted Lady weaving in and out of the azaleas while he was coming out of the town hall building. "Look at her go!"

Dave, a friend who has two English Setters, stopped to say hello to me and admire Lady's bird-hunting skills. We soon struck up a conversation about his dogs, bloodlines and breeding while Lady went about her work. After about 10 minutes, Lady began to get particularly intense, sprinting in about out of the bushes.

"Joe, she's pretty excited about something," Dave said. "It looks like she might have caught a bird in there."

Before I could lean down to look more closely, Lady came charging out of the bushes and dropped from her mouth a 2-inch hairless critter with pointy ears at my feet.

"What is it?" Dave asked.

I got down on my knees to get a closer look. "Oh, wow! It's a baby rabbit, Dave. The eyes are still shut. It's probably only a few days old."

"Look at Lady," Dave said while she proudly panted with delight and joyously wagged her tail. "It looks like she wants you to take it home for her."

And that is exactly what Lady wanted me to do. She had found a baby and wanted to care for it. The infant rabbit, who was faintly grunting, was somehow unharmed. Lady made sure she carried it gently in her mouth. I crawled between the azaleas and could see where Lady had disturbed some leaves on the ground, exposing a small hole with at least three more infant rabbits huddled on top of each other. One had started to work its way out of the den. I grabbed a handkerchief from my pocket and carefully nudged the tiny guy back into the hole. Next, much to Lady's chagrin, I used the handkerchief to pick up the baby that she had dropped at my feet, carried it back to the den and placed the little guy next to its brothers and sisters. The tiny critter's grunts subsided when it felt the contact of its siblings, and I covered up the den with leaves.

During the ensuing days, I made sure that Lady and I kept a safe distance from that clump of azaleas during our daily hikes around Lexington Center. And during one particularly stroll near town hall a few weeks later, we noticed several baby rabbits running around on the grounds and in the shrubs.

Lady may have lost out on bringing home an infant rabbit, but she now had a group of baby rabbits that she could admire while pointing her tail at 12 o'clock during her daily hikes.

A once-favorite stomping ground

Lady's affection for the offspring of wildlife critters went beyond infants. She also admired their toddlers, too. Her maternal instincts were again on full display during a rare hike we made at Willards Woods, Samantha's favorite stomping ground in north Lexington. Since Samantha's death, I had only twice visited this 200-acre conservation area that bustles with wildlife because the heartbreaking image of a gravely ill, elderly Samantha struggling to navigate the trails for the last time just days before her death remained etched foremost in my mind. Instead, I would take Lady and Sampson to Katahdin Woods, a 50-acre conservation area just up the street from our home; to nearby Minuteman National Park; to the town's Old Reservoir and around the Lexington Center area. These were all places that Samantha enjoyed, too.

But on May 1, 2011, the anniversary of Samantha's 15th birthday and a little more than three years since her passing, I had an uncontrollable urge to be at Willards Woods. Even though I was hesitant to go and face that painful image, I decided to take Lady there for a hike. For some inexplicable reason, I had a premonition that something or somebody that I needed to see awaited me at Samantha's favorite stomping ground.

Lady was having fun while she pointed at birds in the bushes and trotted through the fields on this pleasant, sunny afternoon. She would stop and poke her head into every bush looking for birds, the same way Samantha did for so many years. Our hike was turning out to be uneventful, so perhaps my sense about visiting Willards Woods had been wrong. But about 30 minutes into our little journey, Lady opted to drift off the field's main trail onto a less-traveled side path toward an isolated apple orchard. The old orchard, which has a dozen trees, sits on the outskirts of the conservation area. A 15-foot-wide swath of thick grass separates it from a heavily wooded adjacent area of pine, oak and birch trees.

Lady's methodical walk toward the swath of thick grass suddenly jarred my memory. She was walking toward the favorite out-of-the-way spot where Samantha enjoyed lying down and taking a break during our hikes. Oftentimes, I would sit next to her so I could rub her head, neck and shoulders.

An ailing Samantha makes her final trek around Willards Woods in Lexington, her favorite stomping ground, shortly before going over the Rainbow Bridge on April 7, 2008.

Lady carefully approached as if she was looking at a bird, perhaps a pheasant, hiding in the thick grass. She then started to raise her tail to the 12 o'clock position and point. After a few moments, she began happily wagging it. I was about 100 feet away and began to briskly walk toward her to see what she had found. By the time I had gotten there, Lady was panting with delight. This highly focused hunting dog was trying to play with an adolescent raccoon as if it were a puppy. The little guy, perhaps 4 or 5 weeks old, was somewhat nervous but seemed to be enjoying the attention. I quickly pulled Lady away, fearing the raccoon's mother was probably nearby and getting ready to come to the aid of her toddler. Lady, however, would have been content to stay and play with the cute critter.

Lady may have blood coursing through her veins from a long line of champion bird dogs, but even that impressive pedigree is no match against her deep-rooted maternal instincts. And those instincts seem to always rise to the surface whether it be during an unexpected meeting with an adolescent raccoon, while uncovering a den of infant rabbits or when playing at home with her son, Sampson. First and foremost, this bird dog is a tender mom.

A new look at old memories

I have not returned to Willards Woods since that day. Lady's heartwarming encounter with the young raccoon – which would coincidentally occur at Samantha's cherished out-of-the-way resting spot – has recaptured my memories of all the happy times I spent at this special place with my beloved rescue dog. Thanks to Lady's unwavering maternal instincts, the Willards Woods hiking tradition that I shared with Samantha has been restored with a perfect new ending.

Now when I daydream about Samantha and Willards Woods, I shall no longer think about a frail, elderly dog making her final trek around the trail. Instead, I shall remember a youthful, beautiful, happy bird dog snuggling with me in the soft grass next to an orchard while we watched birds peck at apples in the trees.

Chapter 3
The great awakening

The tradition of daily hikes at Willards Wood may have died with Samantha's crossing over to the other side of the Rainbow Bridge, but many of our other customs and rituals, such as the soft kiss I would plant on top of her head each night just before bedtime, would now live on through her grandnephew, Sampson.

Sampson's birth occurred at 11:16 a.m. on April 30, 2010. Starting with that first night, I have given him a peck on the head at bedtime the same way I did each night with his grandaunt. This ritual was my way of reassuring Samantha, a rescue dog, that I would always be there for her, and I wanted to provide Sampson, a singleton puppy, with that same assurance.

> **Starting on Sampson's first day of life, the signals were clear that my home would never be the same with this blossoming boy living in it.**

The newborn puppy had no sense of vision or hearing in those first days of life, but he did have sense of touch. I would routinely rub his neck and back in a gentle, circular motion with two fingers while he was nursing to let him know he would never be alone. I was worried about him being lonely since he had no litter mates. And after about two weeks, when Sampson was becoming sentient, I would whisper "good boy" to him several times a day to build his confidence. Even though Samantha was nearly 3 years old when I adopted her, I did these same things with her during our first few months together to help build a good rapport and strong bond with her. I hoped that the same might happen with Sampson.

I carried on other simple customs, too, such as frequently playing soft classical music on the stereo in the background to create a soothing household environment. Classical music seemed to help the puppy relax in his whelping box the same way it would calm Samantha while she lounged on her bed after a vigorous day of hiking in the fields.

Power and coordination

And this puppy would need relaxation cues such as soothing massage and soft music. Starting on Sampson's first day of life, the signals were clear that my home would never be the same with this blossoming boy living in it. He wasted no time displaying his potential energy and strength. The less-than-one-pound infant surprised me when – only three hours after his birth – he decided to show off his strength by getting up on his hind legs while nursing. Apparently lying on his side lacked excitement, so the tiny guy placed his front legs on Lady's side and began pulling himself up into a partially standing position with his head held high and weight shifted onto his hind legs. He positioned himself upright against his mother's belly with his head nestled almost to the top of her thigh. Lady became concerned about Sampson losing his balance and falling back, so she placed her snout next to him just in case. But he never lost his balance. Sampson remained upright for nearly 15 minutes before eventually tiring, sliding back down and falling asleep.

Sampson's 5-inch length and 12.75-ounce weight at birth were fairly normal for an English Setter, but his power and coordination developed much sooner than the average puppy. At 18 days old, only a few days after opening his eyes, the fully awakened Sampson already had become a feisty puppy who had mastered walking around the whelping box. Normally, a pup at this age would be taking its first wobbly steps. The 23-inch side walls were still too high for him to climb over. Nevertheless, during the next couple of days, the curious little guy would place his front paws on the whelping box's side walls and get up on his hind legs, seeking a spot where he could hoist himself over and escape.

Sampson would soon discover a lower section of the wall that has a removable insert that makes it easier for a mother dog to climb in and out. This part of the wall was only 6 inches high. After observing Lady using this location to leave the whelping box, the curious puppy stood on his back legs with front paws on the 3-inch-wide guardrail that surrounds the inside wall, peering over the shorter wall to see what lurked over the other side. He had determined that this was a potential escape route.

Sampson, less than three hours after his birth, begins his ascent onto his mother's thigh. Normally, a newborn puppy is unable to remain upright, but Sampson used his mother's body for leverage to pull himself up.

First baby steps

Sampson nurses while lying on his belly, left, shortly after his birth. A short time later, the infant puppy shows off his strength by pulling himself up and partially standing on his back legs. Sampson's display gets the attention of Lady, who nuzzles her nose against him to make sure he keeps his balance.

Sampson, looking a little tuckered out from his latest reconnaissance mission, soon sank back down, walked to the middle of the whelping box and decided to nap.

About the 30 minutes later, a reinvigorated Sampson awoke and headed directly to the lower section of the wall. He stood on his hind legs, placed his front paws over the guardrail to reach for the top of the wall and let out a loud grunt. A few seconds later, a louder grunt. And finally, a longer and even louder grunt when he pulled himself over the wall. Sampson fell head over heels onto the soft rug by the kitchen door. He quickly got back on his feet, urinated on the rug and promptly used the same imaginative head-over-heels method to climb back into the whelping box to resume his nap. In only 18 days, this infant had become a bouncing toddler and no longer wanted to soil the place where he slept.

In the ensuing days, Sampson would use his hilariously entertaining head-over-heels method to pull himself out of the whelping box when he needed to toilet. And I would soon replace the rug with fresh newspapers, more fresh newspapers and even more fresh newspapers.

For the acrobatic Sampson, it was time to let the good times flow!

Like mother, like son

The curious toddler continued his explorations during the next few days now that he had mastered getting in and out of the whelping box. And since Sampson had no siblings to help him learn by trial and error, he would take his cues from his mother. He would carefully watch Lady and then emulate her such as he had done to find the easiest route out of the whelping box.

Sampson's next expedition was a step down from the kitchen into the same enclosed entryway where Lady had ferociously confronted pet-sitter Liz Mahoney. I was leaving open the kitchen door that leads into the 4-foot by 6-foot side entryway to let in the warmth from the springtime sunshine. Sampson had been observing his mother leaving the kitchen, going into the entryway and out the door that leads into the yard. So during the next couple of days, the eager-to-learn toddler would repeatedly stand on the edge of the door threshold, measuring whether he could make it down the 7-inch step from the kitchen to the entryway. Finally, at 24 days old, he amassed the courage to jump, making a soft, smooth landing on all four feet. He methodically explored the entryway for several minutes with his nose to the floor. He would find a tennis ball and became fascinated with its ability to roll. After playing with the ball for some time, the tired little guy decided to curl up in a sunny corner and promptly fell asleep.

Sampson's world was rapidly expanding. In a little more than three weeks, he had gone from a helpless infant in a whelping box to an active toddler who possessed the athletic skills to scamper around the kitchen and side porch. I installed pet safety gates in the two kitchen doors that led to the living room to prevent Sampson from getting into the rest of the house. This newfound freedom and tennis ball chasing would only temporarily satisfy Sampson's curiosity. The inquisitive boy had been observing Lady going in and out of the entryway's door that leads into the yard, and he was ready to go on his next journey. But access to the yard requires descending six concrete steps, an impossible task for a now 4-week-old puppy, so I carried the little tyke into the yard where he could spend some time outside with his mother.

Determined boy

A spacious backyard in springtime with soft grass, sprouting flowers and green shrubs provided the perfect backdrop for an energetic, curious bird dog to make his first trek outdoors. Sampson would spend nearly an hour exploring the yard. At times, he would playfully sprint. But for the most part, he would instinctively put his nose to the ground and track the scents, frequently poking his head into the hosta and day lilies growing throughout the yard.

After traversing the yard, the exhausted puppy decided he wanted to go inside. I was about to lift him when he surprised me and quickly moved toward the stairs leading back to the house. He then began pulling himself up the six steps, one by one. I kept both my hands underneath his butt in case he fell back, but the determined little boy just kept grunting while pulling himself up each step until he got to the top.

A skillful puppy

Four-week-old Sampson shows off his coordination and athletic ability by sprinting across our backyard and horsing around with a tennis ball in an enclosed entryway at our home.

During weeks five and six, Sampson would learn to walk down the stairs and into the yard, where he would train with his mother. Lady would spend hours each day helping Sampson hone his innate abilities. The two, working side by side, proficiently pointed at birds in the shrubs, sniffed out critters hiding along the ground in the tall flowers and chased away any chipmunks who dared to stray into their domain.

Lady made time for play, too. Sampson enjoyed playing tug-of-war with a rope toy and especially liked being chased by his mother. Sampson would sprint across the yard, stop short, reverse directions and circle the shrubs. Eventually, Lady would corner him. Using her mouth, she would grab Sampson by one of his back legs and flip him onto his back. The puppy would bark with delight, get up and run away. Soon, the chase would begin again. This routine was repeated multiple times a day, and, with each passing day, Lady was finding it a little more difficult to catch her growing boy.

Advanced skills

The coordination and athleticism of this puppy when he approached 6 weeks old seemed far advanced for his age. And Sampson, who was filled with endless energy, was testing Lady's stamina and my endurance, too. After dinner, an exhausted Lady would sneak off to the living room to get some sleep, having put in a full day of playing and pointing at birds with her puppy. Sampson would then bring his rope toy to me to continue playing tug-of-war and encourage me to go into the yard and chase him. Sometimes, this would go on until sunset and then the fun would resume inside the house until late at night.

Sampson, who a few weeks earlier was a helpless infant who liked to frequently nap, had fully awakened.

Chapter 4
The singleton puppy

Sampson's seemingly superior athletic skills and coordination would be confirmed a few days later during his first visit to Dr. Daria Smith, the primary care veterinarian at Lexington Veterinary Associates who has cared for my English Setters for more than two decades.

After listening to Sampson's heart and checking his body on an examination table, Dr. Smith decided to observe the puppy's coordination and skills. Sampson was placed on the floor and promptly began showing off his athletic abilities, running back and forth along a 15-foot-long hallway.

"This is a very, very healthy puppy," declared Dr. Smith while raising her eyebrows. "He's one of the healthier puppies I've ever seen." As Dr. Smith watched Sampson sniff, track and gracefully move round the hallway, she added:

> **Sampson will always have a unique view of the world because of his lack of litter mates.**

"He's far advanced. He has the skills of a puppy nearly twice his age. He's acting like he's 10 or even 12 weeks old, not six."

Genetics and being healthy at birth played an important role in Sampson's advanced skills, Dr. Smith would later explain, especially since his bloodline is filled with champion field dogs known for their athleticism. "Sometimes, it's just the way they are hard-wired."

But some of Sampson's superior skills are probably attributable to him being a singleton puppy, Dr. Smith said, because he had an endless supply of nourishing mother's milk that helped him grow rapidly in the first few weeks of life. "He had no competition for the milk. He was the only puppy nursing."

The typical litter

Normally, infant puppies have to compete with each other for their mother's milk and her attention, Dr. Smith explained. Puppies are basically helpless during the first two weeks after birth, even needing stimulation to help them urinate from the licks of their mother. And a mother dog has a tendency to pay more attention to the bigger pups who use their strength to get closer to her and grunt the most, resulting in the smaller, weaker ones getting less nutrition and developing slower. "The squeaky wheels get the grease," Dr. Smith said. "Those are the ones that get the most attention."

In addition to gaining an understanding about competition, the puppies also learn essential social skills from each other when they get a little older and become active, Dr. Smith explained. A puppy will learn important lessons about behavior, play and bite inhibition by interacting with its litter mates. Puppies do a lot of nipping when they play, which helps them learn to be careful and gentle, she said. A mother dog also will do some playful biting, but far less than puppies.

A puppy growing up in a litter normally has much better social skills, Dr. Smith said. "They learn how to interact appropriately with other dogs if they are raised with other dogs."

An array of difficulties

According to Dr. Smith, a singleton puppy can face many difficulties, which include: socialization, since it has no siblings to help it learn the nuances of interacting with other dogs; motivation, since it has no competition for milk and its mother's attention; and health, since it can easily become overweight from an endless supply of milk and a lack of exercise due to having no playful siblings.

Obesity can particularly be a major problem, Dr. Smith said, because some singleton pups overindulge on their mother's milk and lack the motivation to play that develops from being part of a litter. This can result in a "swimmer puppy," meaning the pup gets too plump to walk and moves around by crawling and paddling its legs.

Sampson had become pudgy from indulging on an unlimited supply of mother's milk by the time he turned 19 days old. Pups without litter mates can often develop weight problems.

A singleton puppy also can have psychological and emotional issues unlike those raised in a litter, Dr. Smith said. "He has a different viewpoint of the world. He's not used to sharing."

Expectations are even different, Dr. Smith explained. "He expects the food to be there. He expects to be taken care of . ... They just anticipate that they will get what they want. Mom's always going to be there."

Puppies usually are kept with their mother for eight weeks, which is a critical time for them to learn from each other, Dr. Smith said. But a singleton puppy should stay with its mother for 12 weeks. This gives the mother dog extra time to help teach her puppy appropriate behavior.

Sampson's perspective

Sampson faced all these potential problems, especially regarding having his mother's undivided attention and no competition for food. Lady was producing enough milk for an entire litter rather than one puppy. At one point, she even had to have some of the excess liquid manually pumped out at her reproductive veterinarian's office. Even the rapid-growing, plump Sampson, who loved to constantly drink, was unable to consume all the milk.

Lady was certainly making sure her son had more than adequate nutrition and plenty of attention in his first few weeks of life, but she apparently was smart enough to understand Sampson's predicament of being a singleton puppy. In the ensuing critical weeks when Sampson began walking, Lady made sure her pudgy pup got more than adequate exercise by spending hours with him each day in the yard, helping him to hone his bird dog skills every morning and enthusiastically playing with him every afternoon. Many of the afternoon play sessions included wrestling and biting games. Lady fulfilled her motherhood role and was more than willing to take the place of the missing litter mates.

In addition to having a perceptive mother, Sampson had another advantage unafforded to many singleton puppies. He was staying permanently with his mother, which meant his learning and socialization would go on indefinitely. The bond shared by Lady and Sampson would

Lady teaches Sampson about bite inhibition during one of their play sessions. At top, she gently nibbles on Sampson's hind leg. Below, Sampson nips her softly on the lips.

also continue to grow stronger with each passing month. Even after Sampson reached age 1, Lady was still mothering him, socializing him and teaching him how to be a bird dog.

A special Lady

Lady was able to help Sampson overcome potential problems with socialization, motivation and health that affect many singleton puppies, but even a magnificent mother would be unable to alter his perspective about life. Sampson will always have a unique view of the world because of his lack of litter mates. He has some endearing personality quirks that are common in many singleton puppies such as a strong desire to always be the center of attention and the uncontrollable urge to be first in line at dinner time. But thanks to Lady, he avoided all the serious problems that can afflict a singleton puppy.

Sampson is "very fortunate" to have such a good mother, Dr. Smith said. "If he had a different kind of mother, he could have turned out a lot differently."

Lady possesses strong maternal instincts, and she was willing to work hard to help Sampson succeed, Dr. Smith said. Other mother dogs, especially those with weaker maternal instincts, would have been unwilling to put in this kind of effort, she said. "That really helped take the place of the missing puppies. Not all mothers would do that. He has a really exceptional mother."

And one with great wisdom, too.

Chapter 5
Oh boy!

Couch cushions lying on the living room floor have gashes so profound that the inner yellow foam is exposed, woodwork in the kitchen doorway has gouges so deep that the white paint on it has disappeared and a bed blanket has rips so wide that it can barely hold together in one piece.

All are remnants of Sampson's puppy shenanigans during the first year of his life, symbols of the frustrating, yet thoroughly entertaining, trail that I was traveling on with him. This fun-loving, attention-seeking puppy had been wreaking havoc around the house, especially when he went through the teething stage.

I had been accustomed to dealing with female English Setters, such as Dancer, Samantha and Lady, who were adults and played in a more gentle way. I was unprepared to handle Sampson, a rowdy male puppy who loves to wrestle and knock over any object in his path. I had no experience teaching the ways of family life to a rambunctious boy who likes playing tug-of-war and keep-away with every toy, piece of clothing or household item he can get into his mouth.

> **Sampson's mischievous ways and roughhousing had turned our once-quiet, organized home into a den of disorder.**

The art of roughhousing

Sampson's amusing head-over-heels technique of exiting his whelping box during his infant days was a prelude for his roughhousing style. The puppy had no siblings, so he would use objects to entertain himself. He first started doing this with his baby-blue blanket when he turned 5 weeks old. The little guy was no longer staying exclusively in his whelping box, so I folded the blanket into quarters to make a bed and placed it on the floor. At first, Sampson enjoyed lying and snuggling on the soft blanket. But soon, the blanket would become his wrestling opponent. This silly boy would jump on the blanket, continuously roll on it and entangle himself. The more I chuckled, the more the flamboyant little guy would roll on the blanket. Eventually, Sampson would untangle himself, stand on the blanket for leverage and use his sharp puppy teeth to rip it. My efforts to tell Sampson "no" when he got a little too rowdy were ignored. He was just having too much fun to listen.

After getting bored with the blanket, Sampson decided to do some roughhousing with the kitchen woodwork, which may have been fun for him but was far less amusing for me. On many nights, I would hear him scratching and biting it. He seemed to sense that the sharp sounds made by his gnawing teeth while they penetrated the wood would draw my attention and force me to get out of bed, giving him some company. I would offer Sampson a chew toy, which he would play with for awhile. But inevitably, he would resume focusing his attention on the woodwork despite my repeated visits to the kitchen throughout the night and pleas of "no."

The woodwork and blanket kept Sampson entertained for awhile, but the singleton puppy's roughhousing would reach new levels when he turned 12 weeks old. He sneaked into the living room, a place he was allowed to enter only while supervised. I had forgotten to put up the safety gate when I went into the basement to check on laundry. In 10 unsupervised minutes and the five more that I witnessed, Sampson had a knockdown, drag-out wrestling match with the two couch cushions. The material covering the cushions was torn in a couple of places and several pieces of yellow foam stuffing – in mouth-sized hunks – were scattered across the floor.

The silly episode was amusing in some ways, but I knew it also had to be used as a teaching opportunity. I pointed at the damaged cushions and sternly said "no," but Sampson just sat there happily panting, proud of his latest roughhousing performance. My protests that day made as much of an impression on him as they did when he chewed woodwork and ripped blankets.

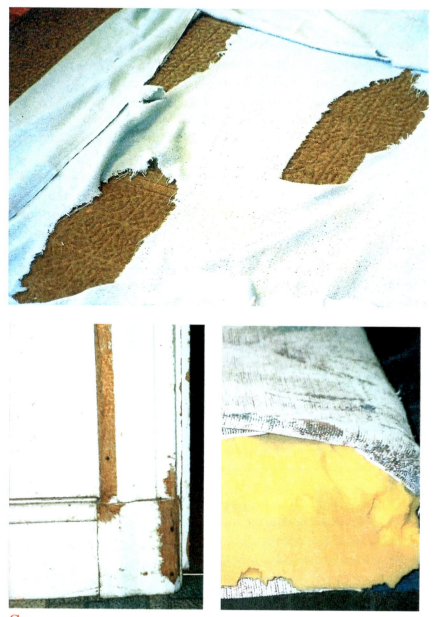

Sampson's puppy shenanigans included ripping his blanket with his teeth, chewing the kitchen woodwork and taking mouth-sized bites from the couch cushions.

For this showboating puppy, the word "no" lacked meaning in his world of fun.

A wise guy

Sampson's desire to play, wrestle and showboat kept growing with his size. His next antics: Stealing my socks, T-shirts and shoes to use for playing keep-away. He would run circles around the house by starting at one end of the kitchen, going through the door to the adjoining living room and coming back through a second door at the opposite end of the kitchen. If I tried chasing him, he would reverse direction, making it impossible to catch him. Years before, Sampson's grandaunt, Samantha, used this same circular route to do a happy, circular dance in anticipation of her food dish being placed on the floor. But the anything-but-dainty Sampson preferred to use the same route to play keep-away.

Sampson was turning into a smart aleck, too, probably a result of being a singleton puppy who always needed to be the center of attention. If I got tired of playing keep-away and stopped chasing, he would tease me by bringing over his toy and waving it at me. He would insist on continuing to play. And despite my efforts to tell him "no" and that it is time to "sleep," this fun-seeking boy would relentlessly taunt me until I would resume the chase.

Sampson was unable, or perhaps unwilling, to take "no" for an answer.

An angel among us

Sampson also had a stubborn streak, which he first began exhibiting during a venture into the yard when he was about 6 weeks old. He started crunching on a stick while I was sitting on the deck. "Sam, no," I yelled. He looked me in the eyes and just kept on chewing the stick. I was concerned about Sampson ingesting parts of the splintering stick, so I got down from the deck, told him "no" while taking the stick and offered him a toy while telling him "good boy."

By the time I had returned to the deck, he would be chewing on another stick. Again I got off the deck, told him "no" while taking the stick and offered Sampson a different toy while telling him "good boy."

After the amusing routine played out for a third time, I realized that Sampson was toying with me in the same way he did while playing keep-away. So I picked up the little devil, carried him onto the deck and put him on my lap. A few moments later, Sampson was exhibiting his softer, delicate side. The precocious puppy was snoozing like an adorable angel in my arms.

My efforts to get Sampson to respond to verbal commands again had been tuned out – literally and figuratively.

Trying times

According to Stanley Coren, a leading canine behaviorist who is a psychologist and professor at the University of British Columbia, the average dog can learn 165 words and has an intelligence level on par with a 2-year-old child.

But Sampson was off to a rough start when trying to learn words. He certainly seemed to understand the word "no" when he kept cunningly grabbing those sticks to get my attention and force me to get off the deck.

Sampson, who was still a young puppy, would need time to learn. Expecting him to learn a large vocabulary at such a young age was unrealistic, so I focused on three phrases: "good boy" to offer praise; "no" for correction; "stay" for control.

The process of teaching Sampson appropriate behavior was tedious, arduous and a little frustrating. I sometimes had difficulty telling the difference between him having trouble understanding and him simply toying with me since he was a clever puppy. But I was determined to help him learn, and each day I would keep attempting to communicate with him. I had no choice but to keep trying.

Double-trouble

Sampson's mischievous ways and roughhousing had turned our once-quiet, organized home into a den of disorder. I had been doing my best to teach him about family life, but I had no prior experience with a puppy, especially a singleton one who wanted constant attention. He was growing up without the benefit of siblings to help him burn off his seemingly endless energy.

By the time Sampson turned 12 weeks old in late July 2010, I was becoming overwhelmed with his stick chewing, woodwork gnawing and blanket tearing. I was losing the battle to train him in family etiquette. Oftentimes, he refused to acknowledge simple commands. The nearly 30-pound Sampson, who was now almost as tall as 40-pound Lady, was getting bigger, stronger and even more active. The playful pup was also tiring out his mother. Six-year-old Lady would be considered a middle-aged mother since many breeders consider ages 2 to 5 to be prime bearing years for English Setters. She was trying her best to keep up with the vigorous boy while we entered the depths of a hot, humid New England summer. This was when Lady would strain her hip from overuse. Our veterinarian, Dr. Smith, had prescribed total rest for 10 days and then a "slow" resumption of activities.

Lady's injury meant that I would have sole responsibility for exercising and entertaining Sampson. But Lady needed special attention, too. She required massages and ice-pack treatments on her ailing hip twice a day. I had double-trouble and needed to find a way to bring harmony to our home. And the essential components to restoring order were improving communication with Sampson and creating safety zones where Lady could rest while her hip injury healed.

Establishing safety zones would be easy. The whelping box in the corner of the kitchen had been replaced four weeks earlier, when Sampson was 8 weeks old, with soft blankets. Lady and Sampson enjoyed lounging on the blankets during the day and sleeping on them at night. I would simply add two large crates, side by side, in that spot and put their blankets and toys inside them. Each dog would now have their own space, where they would be fed and receive treats. Anytime Lady needed privacy, she would be able to go into her crate, and I would shut the access gate.

Sampson was a little unsure about this new arrangement. He disliked being segregated from his mother while she napped in her crate during the day, and he was especially unhappy about being separated at night. Sampson would pull his blanket from his unlocked crate and put it next to the front gate of Lady's crate, where he would sleep in close proximity to his mother. Sampson would soon begin to understand that Lady's crate was her space, and he willingly started to honor her desire to rest. The same arrangement was used with the deck and yard. Lady would go onto the deck when she needed to rest, and Sampson appeared to instinctively understand that his mother needed some private time.

Puppy see, puppy do!

I then had a revelation after observing Sampson's reaction to these changes. The best way to teach him was through Lady. He was clearly responding to the body language and actions of his mother. I had been going about it all wrong. Nonverbal communication was the answer!

I began to ponder about the first few weeks of Sampson's life, recalling how he would keenly observe his mother. At less than 3 weeks old, the newly awakened puppy learned how to exit the whelping box after watching his mother climbing over the wall's lowest point. A few days later, he would learn how to get into the side entryway and eventually into the yard by observing his mother coming in and out of the doors. And, at 4 weeks old, he learned to eat kibble after watching his mother chow down from a bowl placed on the kitchen floor. Sampson had no siblings to help him learn by trial and error. Instead, he learned by emulating his mother.

Sampson's status as a singleton puppy had created a strong dependency with Lady, but he also was continuing to live with his mother while he got older. Puppies frequently are placed in their new homes at 8 weeks old, forcing them to find different role models in a new environment. But 12-week-old Sampson continued to live with his mother, so he instinctively looked to her for guidance.

A mama's boy

Sampson had no siblings, so he took his learning cues from his mother. Above, he eats kibble for the first time at 4 weeks old and, at right, he chows down on morsels of chicken breast. Even when he got older, Sampson continued to emulate his mother. At left, Sampson, at 6 months old, leans over Lady while they watch birds.

I immediately implemented my newfound teaching strategy to help Sampson understand family etiquette. He soon would learn how to be groomed and have his teeth brushed by watching me perform these tasks on Lady. He would eagerly await his turn each night to get groomed and then have his teeth cleaned. Eventually, he even learned to play with his toys a little more gently while he observed Lady playing with me. And he especially liked getting his pink, spotted belly rubbed after watching me stroke his mother's stomach.

A setback

Sampson displayed a strong ability to learn, but he still would revert to his silly stunts at times during his first puppy year. A big regression occurred at 9 months old, when he again sneaked into the living room to finish his wrestling match with the couch cushions. The helpless cushions never stood a chance against the pummeling they would receive from the now 49-pound boy, who was larger than his mother. I found the cushions disassembled. Sampson had ripped the foam into countless mouth-sized balls. I was somewhat disheartened by the transgression, but I took comfort in the fact that Sampson had avoided injury. He could have swallowed some foam and gotten sick.

Despite the setback, Sampson continued learning the ways of family life. Eventually, I began having him observe while I gave Lady verbal signals in the yard. I would have him watch while I told her "no" if she picked up a stick and say "leave it" to instruct her to put it down. He also observed me extending my arm while pointing my finger and telling Lady "this way" for recall and to offer direction. I had figured out the proper way to communicate with Sampson, and he was rapidly learning family etiquette.

Oh boy! I had saved my house from completely going to the dogs.

Chapter 6
A haven for bird dogs

Sampson nervously stands on the shiny metal examination table with his head and shoulders drooping, back legs wobbling and tail curling down between his legs while he awaits the arrival of the veterinarian. But his anxiety is secondary compared to the ache in his belly. The 10-month-old puppy with a ferocious appetite had vomited that morning and refused to eat.

"He seems to have an upset stomach," I told Dr. Smith, our primary care veterinarian at Lexington Veterinary Associates, when she entered the room. "He ate fine two nights ago, but yesterday he barely ate at all."

Dr. Smith began examining Sampson, first looking at his eyes and ears before using her stethoscope to listen to his belly.

> **I needed to create a backyard designed exclusively for bird dogs.**

"Maybe he needs something to settle his stomach," I suggested while she rubbed her hands along Sampson's abdomen.

"I feel something," Dr. Smith said. "There's a lump."

My legs, like Sampson's, were now wobbling after hearing the word lump. After losing Samantha three years earlier to cancer, I was terrified about the possibility that Dr. Smith had found a tumor and my beloved puppy was going to die.

"Oh, no!" I screamed. "He's just a baby. He deserves to have a long life. How can he have cancer? How can this be happening?"

"No, no. It's nothing like that," said Dr. Smith, trying to calm me while taking my hand and moving it along Sampson's stomach so I could feel the lump. "I think he swallowed something," she said. "You need to get him to the hospital right away. They need to do an ultrasound to figure out exactly what's in there."

Sampson's discomfort was likely being caused by whatever he swallowed, Dr. Smith explained, and "it needs to come out right way."

Moments later, Sampson and I would begin a 15-minute drive to Massachusetts Veterinary Referral Hospital in neighboring Woburn. Shortly after arriving, Sampson was examined by Dr. Heidi White, who also rubbed her hands along Sampson's abdomen. Dr. White, who had been told of the findings made at Lexington Veterinary Associates, agreed that Sampson had likely swallowed a foreign object.

"Unfortunately, we see this all the time," she said, assuring me that the likelihood of a tumor was remote. "Puppies are always putting things in their mouths and accidentally swallowing them."

The object's location in Sampson's intestinal tract was discernible by touch, but Dr. White ordered an ultrasound of his abdomen to confirm the spot and to make sure "nothing else is in there."

I anxiously waited while Sampson was brought into a nearby testing room. The ultrasound would reveal a sole object, pinpointing its location. The walnut-sized item was near Sampson's small intestine, and he would need emergency surgery to remove it.

"Can you tell what this thing is?" I asked.

"We won't know until the surgeon removes it," Dr. White responded.

A couple of hours later, Sampson was resting comfortably in the recovery room following successful surgery. The mystery foreign object turned out to be piece of material from a T-shirt that Sampson had heisted from a laundry basket in my bedroom a couple of days earlier.

Sampson and Lady had been playing tug-of-war with it in our backyard. Sampson must have torn off a piece of the shirt and accidentally swallowed it while they were playing.

Sampson and Lady play tug-of-war with a T-shirt that the mischievous 10-month-old pup, who now was larger than his mother, had swiped from a laundry basket.

"The material somehow rolled itself into a ball while it was passing through his stomach," Dr. White explained. "It got stuck when it was entering his small intestine and blocked his digestive tract."

Sampson's rambunctious ways had finally caught up with him.

Where did I go wrong?

My puppy would spend the next three days recovering at the hospital. During my visits to comfort him, I thought about all the precautions I had taken inside our home to keep Sampson safe since that first day he did his head-over-heels flip from the whelping box onto the kitchen floor.

In the kitchen, where Sampson primarily stayed, a safe zone had been created by removing all items that a puppy might find appealing to use as toys. Electrical cords near the floor were taken away, cords on the window blinds were spiked down to the wall to prevent them from dangling and plug outlets had been covered. Even the plastic tip on the metal doorstop was removed to prevent Sampson from pulling it off and ingesting it. And pet safety gates kept him confined to the kitchen. Other areas of the house, such as the living room, were off-limits unless Sampson was being supervised by me.

Yet, Sampson still ended up at a hospital, where he would have to have emergency surgery to remove a foreign object. I asked myself: "Where did I go wrong?"

The obvious answer to my question was indicative of my inexperience with puppies. I had overlooked the one place, other than the puppy-proofed kitchen, where Sampson spent most of his time. I had neglected to make modifications to the backyard. After Sampson turned 6 weeks old, much of his rambunctious play occurred outside. He would spend many hours every day in the 50-foot by 40-foot fenced area. Sampson enjoyed watching birds, but he seemed to enjoy roughhousing even more in an open space that encouraged disorderly play. And during the winter of 2010, which was Sampson's first, we had an abundance of snow that made the yard even more inviting for his roughhousing. The snow banks and maze of shoveled paths made it perfect for Sampson to play tug-of-war and keep-away with Lady.

The yard, where it was more difficult for me to monitor Sampson's activities, needed to be made as safe as the house's interior. But how? Removing every rock, stick, toy or object that he could ingest was impossible, and keeping vigil over him also was unrealistic. So the only solution would be a behavioral change. Sampson needed to focus on something other than roughhousing.

But slowing this boy down would be a difficult task. In addition to spending hours in the yard, I was taking Sampson on hikes each day in the fields to allow him to expend some of his endless puppy energy. Sampson, being a bird dog from a long line of champions, loved pointing at birds and chasing critters during our hikes. But those miles-long hikes were failing to tire him out, so he would go back to the yard and want to roughhouse with Lady.

All critters welcome

Sampson needed to be in an environment that would touch the core of his existence and stimulate his instincts, so I needed to create a backyard designed exclusively for bird dogs. The focus would change from growing green grass and pretty flowers to fulfilling the needs of Lady and Sampson. Their happiness, rather than backyard cosmetics, would take priority. And keeping these bird dogs entertained and satisfied meant attracting a steady stream of wildlife, especially birds.

The backyard already had many natural characteristics that could be used to help create a favorable environment for bird dogs and to attract wildlife. A small meadow-like area surrounded by eight towering pine trees, some as high as 60 feet, sits just outside the rear of the house. And under those pines, the many shrubs would make nice perches for birds. Those lilac, forsythia and yew evergreen bushes are complemented by fern and vinca flowers that create a thick ground cover ideal for small critters. The backyard also slopes downward from the house, creating a nice venue at the top of the yard to watch wildlife activity in the trees, shrubs, ground cover and the little meadow.

Mother Nature had generously provided, so now it was up to me to enhance those indigenous features to create a haven where wildlife and bird dogs could coexist. As the snow melted and we entered the spring of 2011, I formulated a plan for the transformation. The ground directly under the pine trees beyond the fenced-in small meadow would be left unsullied to allow the fern and vinca flowers to grow taller and thicker. A yew shrub at the corner of the yard next to the house would be allowed to grow wider and more shrubs would be planted in the middle of the yard. And lastly, the most important improvement would be the addition of two strategically-placed bird feeders.

A game plan

One bird feeder would hang from the side of the deck and the other would sit on a 6-foot stand halfway down the sloping yard toward the right side just below a low branch on one of the pine trees. It would be about 15 feet from the deck that overlooks the yard and 25 feet from the adjacent stairs that lead into the yard. The stairs would be at the same eye level with this bird feeder and the deck would be slightly higher, making them perfect venues for Lady and Sampson to watch birds eating seed. The dogs also could sit under the elevated deck to conceal themselves from the birds. Centrally locating the bird feeders also would create flight corridors for the birds, who liked to perch on the lilac bush on one side of the yard and the yew evergreen on the other.

The birds would have their feeders and the critters would have their tall brush under the pine trees, but the yard still had a major problem. Lady and Sampson had trampled all the grass within the fenced area. The lack of grass had created a dust bowl during the previous summer, a slippery ice slope during the winter and now a muddy mess during the spring. Instead of trying to grow grass, a bed of playground quality wood chips would be spread on the ground in the fenced area. These wood chips, which are frequently used beneath children's swing sets, are smooth and do not splinter. They would make a soft, clean foundation for the dogs.

Let the show begin!

I began transforming the yard in late April, around the time Sampson would celebrate his first birthday, and the project was completed a few weeks later. At first, only a few birds were pecking at the feeders. But by the time May had turned to June, birds were flocking to eat in our yard. A steady stream of chirping sparrows, chickadees and cardinals began navigating regular flight paths across the yard from the yew evergreen to the feeders. Soon after, others were making dive-bombing runs from lower branches of the pine trees. Cooing mourning doves would soon join the flight parade, landing under the feeders to feast on seed that had fallen to the ground. And the birds would be followed by chipmunks and field mice, who were also looking for seed along the ground. The sight of birds, chipmunks and mice eating alongside each other on the ground below the feeders became commonplace. The birds and critters were gorging themselves so much that I had to replenish the feeders each morning.

Lady would quickly take notice of the yard's new visitors. As an experienced bird dog, she sought out the best venues to watch the show. She liked sitting at the top of the stairs and on the elevated area under the deck next to the stairs. Sampson would soon become enthralled with the wildlife after observing Lady watching, pointing and stalking birds. Observing critters quickly began to replace roughhousing. As the summer progressed, the ground cover under the pine trees grew thicker and taller. Eventually, rabbits and groundhogs were sneaking into the fenced area to look for seed on the ground below the bird feeders. Lady and Sampson would hide under the deck, wait for them to get near the feeders and then chase them off.

Don't gobble the food

But the true testament to the backyard's transformation would come in the autumn of 2011, when six wild turkeys decided to visit. Turkeys are plentiful in nearby Katahdin Woods, but they had previously never entered our yard. Lady and Sampson, who were inside the house resting, nearly broke down the door when they heard the sound of gobbles coming from the yard. They ran down the walkway and stopped at the top of the stairs, where they began pointing while they watched the turkeys pecking away below in our yard. After a minute of pointing and observing, the temptation was too great for them to hold their ground. They charged down into the yard after the unsuspecting birds.

Bird's-eye view

A balcony-like deck and a landing at the top of the stairs make perfect venues for watching birds and an assortment of other wildlife that come to eat at the feeders in our yard. At top, Sampson and Lady look down into the yard. At left, Sampson gazes into the trees. At right, Lady watches birds gorge on seed at a feeder.

A wild turkey prepares to munch on birdseed that has fallen on to the ground from a feeder in our backyard.

The turkeys began running in multiple directions while the dogs pursued them. Two jumped over the back fence, another ran across the yard before hopping over the side fence and into a neighbor's yard, two flew into the pine trees and the last one took refuge on our house's roof. It kept trying to hide behind the chimney when Lady and Sampson would look up at it. The dogs would angle themselves to see the turkey, and the terrified bird would move to the opposite side of the chimney to get out of sight. This sideshow went on for nearly a half-hour before the turkey gained enough confidence to fly from the roof and into the nearby pines to hide with the other two that initially flew into the trees.

Lady and Sampson were so entertained by the daily shows being put on by Mother Nature's critters that they found little time for roughhousing. Occasionally, they would play keep-away with a toy or chase each other around. But each day the wildlife just kept coming back for encores, and Lady and Sampson would quickly get into their front-row seats at the top of the stairs or on the deck.

In this bird-dog entertainment center, the show must go on.

Chapter 7
One dog, two worlds

Sampson, even though he is only 8 weeks old and just 14 pounds, shows no fear while he instinctively raises his tail to the 12 o'clock position and points at a 3-foot-tall wild turkey that towers over him during a hike at Katahdin Woods. A day later, the puppy is whimpering and lying on his belly with his front paws on top of his head while a tiny bee buzzes above him during a hike at the Old Reservoir in Lexington.

Welcome to the two worlds of Sampson. He is a fearless bird dog on one day and a frightened family pet on the next day.

Learning to live in these conflicting worlds would be a challenge for Sampson. His grandaunt, Samantha, was a bird dog who was able to seamlessly adapt to family life when she came to live with me. But she was a nearly 3-year-old adult dog when I adopted her and the only pet in the household. Sampson was a highly impressionable singleton puppy taking his cues from a mother raised in a hunting environment whose only taste of family life had come in the year she had lived with me prior to Sampson's birth. Lady was helping Sampson develop his natural bird-dog abilities, but she lacked the necessary skills to teach her puppy about the nuances of family life. She was still learning how to balance these worlds herself.

> **Sampson had to learn that he could be rough while tracking on the trails, but he needed to be gentle while playing with people.**

In addition to having to balance the challenges of being a bird dog and family pet, Sampson was also dealing with the intricacies of being a singleton puppy. I was concerned that the conflicting demands of these worlds might be overwhelming and stressful for a singleton puppy from a bloodline filled with champion bird dogs. Would Sampson be able to understand that it is permissible to pursue a turkey during a hike in the woods but inappropriate to dig a hole under the backyard fence to get at a bird on the other side? He had many obstacles to overcome.

A fierce bird dog

Sampson's bird-dog instincts began to surface during his first foray into our backyard. The 4-week-old puppy's desire to play was secondary to his interest in looking at the birds in the bushes. And those instincts quickly expanded to encompass all critters, including his initial encounters with a chipmunk and a rabbit in Katahdin Woods when he turned 6 weeks old.

During the rendezvous with the rabbit, Sampson showed off his hereditary stalking skills. The curious puppy slowly approached the bunny as it ate grass in a yard bordering Katahdin Woods. As Sampson got closer, the rabbit moved back a few feet toward the woods. Sampson would then resume his deliberate approach. This cat-and-mouse routine played out four times until the rabbit, getting more nervous each time Sampson pursued, decided to run off into the depths of woods.

And during the meeting with the chipmunk, Sampson displayed his determination. First, he chased it into a long rock wall that runs through the woods. Then, the puppy kept poking his nose into the crevices between the stones, trying to flush out the critter. As Sampson approached, the chipmunk would make a high-pitched chirp. And each time it made the sound, Sampson would pull down the smaller rocks with his paws to try to get at it. After about 20 minutes, I picked up a tired Sampson and brought him out of the woods after it became apparent that he would indefinitely continue his pursuit.

At only 6 weeks old, Sampson was pointing, tracking and flushing.

Sampson's legs began getting quite long in proportion to his body when he got a little older, a physical characteristic that he inherited from his long-legged mother. By the time the puppy turned 6 months old, he stood at about 22 inches from shoulder to the ground, about the same size as Lady, and much of his height was attributable to his legs.

Sampson, at 6 months old, had legs that were quite long in proportion to his body. His lengthy legs make it easier for him to chase down birds and other critters.

And those lengthy legs would give Sampson extra speed and jumping ability, which he put to good use while chasing birds in the fields and in our backyard. He would stand at the top of the steps, sprint into the yard when he saw a bird flying down from the trees and jump into its flight path while it headed toward the feeder. The birds almost always avoided Sampson, who would sometimes spend hours pursuing them. But on a few occasions, Sampson jumped high enough to grab a bird in flight with his mouth. The proud puppy would then bring the bird to me.

Whether on the trails or in the backyard, this budding bird dog was all heart.

A family pet

Sampson's bird-dog instincts were impressive, but another part of him, an affinity for people that made his grandaunt, Samantha, so special, also began to emerge in him at a young age. He loved being cuddled from the moment he first opened his eyes about two weeks after his birth. Even during his first daily hikes when he was a 6-week-old puppy, Sampson made time to warmly greet people and other dogs. One moment, he would be sniffing around like a bird dog; the next moment, he was playing with children and other dogs. Just like Samantha, Sampson seemed to be able to turn from a highly focused bird dog into a loving family pet as fast as a humming bird can flap its wings.

Sampson's affection for people was as strong as his burning desire to point at birds. Playing with squeaky toys, chasing a ball and curling up on his bed quickly became part of his daily routine. This personality trait in Samantha's side of the bloodline that breeder Michael Ryba and his Connecticut hunting friends had worked hard to instill in their bird dogs in the 1980s and 1990s was emerging in Sampson. And his playful, family-oriented demeanor actually began to rub off on his mother. Lady began to notice the enjoyment her puppy was having playing with squeaky toys and balls, and she soon would decide to participate in the fun.

Sampson possessed natural family skills, but he still needed to understand that playing with people and working on the trails required different uses of his energy and strength. Sampson had to learn that he could be rough while tracking on the trails, but he needed to be gentle while playing with people.

Balancing two worlds

And Sampson's first lesson, and perhaps the most important, occurred in early July 2010 when he was 8 weeks old. The Lexington area was in the throes of a hot, muggy spell, so Sampson and I were taking our daily walks around the Old Reservoir. The shade from the trees and a light breeze off the water made the summer heat a little more tolerable. This quaint place, unlike other hiking venues around town, also gave Sampson the opportunity to interact with people who go to the swimming hole to suntan on the beach and cool off in the water. During one particular walk, Sampson was approached by a 4-year-old boy, who was eager to pat him.

"Is it OK for my son to pat your puppy?" the child's father asked. "He just loves dogs."

"Absolutely," I responded.

"This is Sampson," I said to the child. "He's a very young boy just like you."

The child and Sampson made an immediate connection. The boy had an ear-to-ear grin while he rubbed Sampson's shoulders and back, and Sampson panted with delight. But after a few minutes, a bird flying overhead distracted Sampson. He turned suddenly to get a look. Even though Sampson was only 14 pounds, the force of him quickly turning and bumping his body against the boy's legs caused the child to fall on his butt in the soft sand. The startled boy was unhurt, but he began crying from fright.

"Oh, I'm so sorry," I said to the father. "I don't want your son to be afraid of dogs."

Playful pup

Sampson may be an intense bird dog, but here the 18-month-old pup shows his playful side while he chews on a rubber squeaky toy with prongs while lying on the couch. At right, he runs around the living room with a toy that once had four dangling 6-inch straps before he tore them off.

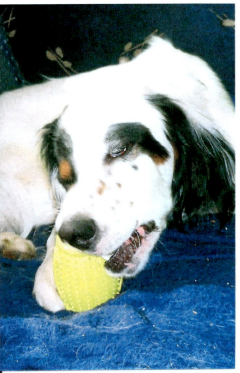

"He's OK," the father assured me while he helped the child back onto his feet.

Sampson, noticing the tears and sensing the child was frightened, proceeded to surprise the child's father and me by getting down on his belly in a passive sphinx position. The puppy had instinctively assumed a non-threatening posture so the child could resume patting him.

"Did you teach him how to do that?" the father asked.

"No," I responded. "This is the first time I've seen him do that. He just did it on his own."

"That's quite a puppy you have there," the father said.

"He sure is," I proudly responded.

A gentle soul

The encounter with the boy at the Old Reservoir was the beginning of a behavioral pattern for Sampson. After the mishap, Sampson began to greet children and small dogs by getting down in his sphinx position. And this non-threatening technique would serve him well when he got larger. By October of 2010, the small puppy had become a 6-month-old, 43-pound muscular boy, and most dogs he was meeting during his daily hikes were smaller than him. But as the big puppy slowly edged closer to adulthood, he just kept getting more and more gentle around children and smaller dogs. His demeanor as a fierce bird dog from a bloodline of champions was simply no match for the innate people-oriented personality trait that he shares with his paternal ancestors.

Sampson may have been born with the heart of a bird dog, but he possessed the soul of a family pet.

Chapter 8
Physical and mystical

A square-shaped white forehead, a tricolor face highlighted by chestnut eyes and an oval-shaped black patch on the lower back. All are unmistakable physical characteristics of Samantha's bloodline, and Sampson has them all.

Sampson looks a lot like his father, Zor, and his paternal grandaunt, Samantha, but that strong family resemblance was slow to emerge. He resembled Lady and the maternal side of his bloodline during the first 6 months of his life. Initially, Sampson was long-legged and sleek, just like his mother.

> **Sampson began to exhibit some of Samantha's unique mannerisms when he approached age 1.**

The big, eye-catching black patch on the lower back of Sampson's predominately white body was the only discernible physical trait he had from the paternal side of his bloodline when he was born. The patch is almost identical to one on Samantha's back. Mickey, who was Sampson's paternal great-great-great-grandfather, had the same patch. Sampson's physical characteristics from the paternal side of his bloodline would gradually develop with age. At 6 months old, black ticking would begin to show on his white legs that would become brown at his ankles and feet; at 9 months old, black speckles and brown speckles began to appear on his white cheeks; and at 12 months old, the hair on his throat and behind his legs began to get long and silky. All were traits that Sampson shared with Samantha. He even has Samantha's smile as well as her droopy side lips, which cause lots of drooling.

Speed and power

Sampson was looking more and more like Samantha and Zor when he approached age 1, but then big changes started to occur from age 12 months to 18 months. That is when his shoulders began to broaden and muscles started to thicken. In the 1990s, Michael Ryba, Samantha's breeder, had carefully mated his dogs to produce larger, more powerful field Setters. According to the North American Llewellin Breeders Association, male field Setters typically weigh close to 50 pounds. But Mike wanted to add another 5 to 10 pounds of muscle to his dogs, believing the extra strength would make these athletic dogs better hunters. The dogs in Mike's bloodline, such as Samantha and Zor, are muscular with wide shoulders, yet they have maintained their exceptional speed and agility. And those paternal genes began to emerge in Sampson when he got closer to adulthood. His body shape was changing from sleek to powerful.

Sampson's development into a powerhouse bird dog is no surprise even though he has a sleek mother. His ability to get up onto his hind legs only three hours after birth, his acrobatic head-over-heels method of exiting his whelping box at 18 days old and his sprinting skills at 4 weeks old were all clues of his athleticism and emerging superior strength.

A wild-goose chase

And that speed and exceptional power were never more evident than during a vigorous morning trek when he was 8 months old in December 2010. Sampson and I were walking on a quiet Sunday morning near the soggy, muddy stadium at Lexington High School, where a couple dozen geese were grazing in a particularly swampy section at the far side. The fenced-in stadium, which has a football field and a baseball field, is off-limits to dogs, but nobody had bothered to tell that to rambunctious Sampson. We were moving past the open gates when Sampson, who you might say was still learning the finer points of walking on a 16-foot retractable leash hooked to a shoulder harness, made a sudden dash toward the stadium. This energetic boy was moving extremely fast, making it impossible for me to lock the leash before he reached its end. The leash, which supposed to be strong enough to restrain a dog up to 110 pounds, was no match for Sampson. The powerful, now 46-pound pup ripped it right out of its holding cartridge.

Sampson was now hot on the trail of the geese and nothing – verbal commands from me, the distraction of a 16-foot leash dragging behind him nor mud splashing in his face – was going to dissuade the determined puppy from trying to catch those birds. Sampson raced across the football field like a sprinting running back trying to reach the goal line with defenders in close pursuit. The silly birds, apparently underestimating Sampson's speed, initially started to honk and jog from the far end zone toward the baseball field, splashing water and mud onto themselves during their haste to get away. Sampson, who sprinted nearly 100 yards in about 7 seconds, got to within 10 yards of the mud-covered geese, who realized it was time to either fly or die.

Sampson had shown off his power by ripping the leash from its cartridge and his speed while dashing nearly 100 yards. Now, he was prepared to show off his athleticism. The honking birds flew in circles over the stadium looking for a safe place to land while Sampson ran below them. Despite my repeated pleas to "stay," he kept racing up, down and across the fields for about 20 minutes while the geese flew above. Sampson put on a dazzling display of agility, smoothly pivoting and changing direction while running at top speed on the soggy fields to stay in lockstep with the geese while they circled in the sky. They were trying to tire out Sampson, so he would stop chasing them. They were hoping to land and reclaim their spot on the football field. But the frustrated birds finally gave up and flew away after realizing that Sampson would never stop his relentless pursuit. The exhausted puppy, who was covered in mud from head to tail, then plopped down to rest and cool off in a puddle at the 50-yard line of the football field while watching the geese disappear into the distant sky.

The birds may have been foolish to think that they could outlast Sampson, but, in the end, this determined, agile and powerful boy was the one who wound up in a mud puddle looking like a silly goose.

Here we go again

Sampson had many similarities with Samantha, including exceptional physical strength, body shape and markings, when he approached adulthood. He also possessed the same family-oriented personality, which featured the ability to shift from focused bird dog to loving pet in a moment. The physical likeness and personality traits can easily be explained by genetics and upbringing, but the similarities went beyond physical and personality. Sampson began to exhibit some of Samantha's unique mannerisms when he approached age 1.

During the winter of 2010-2011, when Sampson was about 9 months old, he began a nightly sleeping routine identical to the one Samantha followed on cold nights. Samantha would start out snoozing on her bed, seemingly in a deep sleep. But each time the oil furnace would fire up in the basement, she would get up from her bed, stroll across the house and lie on the floor in front of the heat vent in the kitchen. She would rest there while the warm air from the furnace comforted her. And when the furnace turned off and the warm air stopped flowing, she would return to her bed. Samantha would repeat this routine throughout the night, returning to the spot on the floor in front of the kitchen heat vent every time she heard the rumble of the furnace. And now, Sampson was following the same routine.

Initially, I attributed the wintertime sleeping routine shared by Samantha and Sampson to mere happenstance. But my sense of deja vu would only deepen during the first winter of Sampson's young life. He soon would start to perform another one of Samantha's favorite routines. One morning, Sampson approached me when I was sitting in a bedroom chair and putting on my slippers shortly after I had gotten out of bed. He began repeatedly rubbing his side and back against my lifted right foot in a catlike manner. This was the same way Samantha greeted me each morning for many years.

I had been willing to write off the wintertime sleeping routine to happenstance, but Sampson's instinctive morning greeting had piqued my curiosity. The catlike rubbing against a person, which is an abnormal behavior for most dogs, was too much of a coincidence for me to ignore.

Heavenly guidance

Sampson's desire to rub against my foot and sleep in front of the kitchen heat vent in the same way that Samantha had done for so many years got me thinking about my dear longtime friend and spiritual adviser, the late Rev. Bruce T. Robb, and his theory about coincidence. Our friendship spanned for decades, dating back to our days at college.

Sampson lies on the kitchen floor in the path of hot air flowing from the vent in the same way Samantha did for many years.

Rev. Robb had served several years as the pastor of the Preston Hollow Baptist Church in Preston Hollow, New York, before passing away at the far too young age of 48 in 2006. He believed that "coincidence is God's way of remaining anonymous in the world while directing events."

I began to reminisce about the many coincidences that occurred throughout Samantha's life, which include:

- My discovery that Michael Ryba was my dog's breeder on my mother's 81st birthday, April 30, 2008, which occurred only hours before what would have been Samantha's 12th birthday on May 1.

- Lady defying overwhelming odds and giving birth to a single puppy rather than the normal litter of 6 to 8 pups for an English Setter – a surprising event explained by Dr. Frances Paulin, the Connecticut veterinarian who helped Zor and Lady mate, simply as "an act of God."

- Sampson's birth occurring on April 30, 2010, precisely two years to the day that I learned Mike Ryba was the breeder of Samantha and on the very day marking the 83rd birthday of my deceased mother, the person who gave me my love of animals.

The Rainbow Bridge

I had assumed these mystical episodes and the many others that occurred during Samantha's life and shortly after her death had ended with Sampson's birth. But, in reality, the coincidences had only taken a short hiatus before resuming. Sampson's routine of sleeping in front of the kitchen heat vent and his rubbing against my foot began in January 2011, about nine months after his birth. And the sweet encounter that Lady had with the adolescent raccoon at Willards Woods in the same spot where Samantha enjoyed lounging in the grass next to the old apple orchard occurred on May 1, 2011, on the day marking Samantha's 15th birthday and just a couple of months after Sampson had started emulating some of Samantha's favorite routines. These events had gotten my attention, and I could only speculate about their possible meaning based on Rev. Robb's theory about God and coincidence. Was this God's way of letting me know that Samantha is in good hands on the other side of the Rainbow Bridge while she awaits our inevitable reunification? Or could these surprising events simply be attributed to happenstance?

I wanted to believe the events were a form of communication, but I was unsure. I have no doubt about God's guiding hand being involved in Samantha's mystical journey through life based on the many coincidences that occurred during her lifetime and after her death leading up to Sampson's birth. Those incidents were too dramatic to be attributed to chance. But these latest coincidences were somewhat subtle, so a part of me remained skeptical.

Sampson's emulation of Samantha's routine of sleeping in front of the kitchen heat vent could simply be a case of a smart dog figuring out the best way to keep warm on cold winter nights. And his desire to rub up against my foot like Samantha could possibly be just a matter of chance. Although uncommon, some dogs do like to rub against people in a catlike manner. But Lady's wonderful encounter with the young raccoon at Willards Woods is more difficult to attribute to happenstance since it occurred on what would have been Samantha's 15th birthday and on the very spot that Samantha and I had spent many days lounging in the grass next to the old apple orchard watching birds.

Coincidences come to a crawl

Sampson continued to regularly rub against my foot in the mornings throughout the summer of 2011 and again began to sleep in front of the kitchen heat vent when the furnace began kicking on when the New England nights cooled in October. I enjoyed having these reminders of Samantha, even though I remained unsure if the coincidences had any deeper, mystical meaning. I would get more clarity in late October 2011 when another unexpected coincidence occurred. During a walk on a lovely, sunny autumn day, Sampson abruptly plopped down on the soft grass in front of the Hancock United Church of Christ, a Congregational parish on the outskirts of Lexington Center. He got into a sphinx position with his belly against the ground and back legs extended straight out like a frog.

This positioning of the rear legs is somewhat uncommon for a dog, who must have excellent dexterity in its hips to be able to fully extend them at 180 degrees. Sampson has outstanding athletic skills, so I was not surprised that he could get into this pose. He then curled all four feet and dug his toes into the ground. He began pulling himself with his front legs while pushing himself with his back legs, crawling like a commando. He methodically moved about 25 feet with his belly and chest rubbing along the soft grass.

Sampson was crawling along in the same unique manner like Samantha! His grandaunt loved to do the commando crawl in the snow and grass, and she especially liked to do it at Lexington's Old Reservoir. Samantha had become well-known for her water escapades. Rather than swim, she would get down on her stomach in the shallow water just off the shore, covering herself up to her neck. She then would do the commando crawl for about 100 feet along the shoreline. On some occasions, she would go back and forth several times. Now, 18-month-old Sampson was instinctively performing the commando crawl that I thought had ended with the passing of Samantha.

A desire to perform

A woman, who was walking by with her young son, spotted Sampson while he was doing the commando crawl. "Oh, that's so cute. He's absolutely adorable," she said. Sampson, noticing that he now had an audience, continued to crawl back and forth across the church lawn to the delight of the child. "Wow, that's so unusual," the mother said. "I didn't know dogs could do that."

And Sampson, who loved to showboat, began doing the commando crawl faithfully during our daily walks, especially when he sensed that people were watching. By the time autumn had turned to winter, he was performing in the snow.

"That's really funny," an amused teenage boy said while watching Sampson pull himself around in the snow in the middle of Depot Square in Lexington Center. "I've never seen a dog do that. Have you?" the teenager asked.

Sampson does the commando crawl in the snow. He faithfully performs this unusual routine, a favorite of Samantha, each day during our walks.

"Only one other dog," I responded while smiling. "His grandaunt used to do the exact same thing."

Lexington resident Joan Rutila, who owns a rescue hound-mix by the name of Rosie, also got to see Sampson perform the commando crawl in the snow in front of Cary Memorial Library in Lexington Center. "That's really unique," Joan said while watching Sampson.

Joan, who owned another rescue dog named Chance prior to getting Rosie, has been walking daily with her dogs around Lexington for many years and encounters many other people walking their dogs. "I've never seen another dog do anything like that," she said.

Someone's watching over us

Sampson has continued to do the commando crawl on his daily walks to the delight of onlookers. And every time he does, I ask myself: How is it possible that he can be performing this uncommon routine mastered by a grandaunt who went over to the other side of the Rainbow Bridge before he was even born? Why would he be doing this unusual routine since he had never seen it before?

I know what Rev. Robb would tell me if he were here.

My mystical journey that began when I adopted a tranquil rescue dog named Samantha has gone on for more than a dozen years. It is now moving forward with her rambunctious grandnephew who loves to wrestle with his blanket, rip apart couch cushions and flop in fields of mud. Sampson also continues to faithfully sleep in front of the kitchen heat vent, rub against my foot and do the commando crawl. And who knows how many more boisterous episodes and heartwarming "coincidences" lie ahead on this captivating trail that I am traversing with this unique boy?

God only knows.

Sampson takes a well-deserved rest after doing the commando crawl in the snow.

Sampson points at a bird in our yard. The singleton pup had become a handsome adult bird dog when he reached age 2.

Made in the USA
Middletown, DE
04 December 2020